A QUICK GUIDE TO

Teaching Second-Grade Writers
with Units of Study

Other Books in the Workshop Help Desk Series

A Quick Guide to
Reaching Struggling Writers, K–5
M. COLLEEN CRUZ

A Quick Guide to
Teaching Persuasive Writing, K–2
SARAH PICARD TAYLOR

A Quick Guide to
Making Your Teaching Stick, K–5
SHANNA SCHWARTZ

A Quick Guide to
Boosting English Acquisition in Choice Time, K–2
ALISON PORCELLI AND CHERYL TYLER

For more information about these and other titles,
visit www.firsthand.heinemann.com.

A QUICK GUIDE TO
Teaching Second-Grade Writers with Units of Study

LUCY CALKINS

Workshop Help Desk Series

Edited by Lucy Calkins

with the Teachers College Reading and Writing Project

DEDICATED TO TEACHERS™

HEINEMANN

Portsmouth, NH

An imprint of Heinemann

361 Hanover Street
Portsmouth, NH 03801–3912
www.heinemann.com

Offices and agents throughout the world

Library of Congress Cataloging-in-Publication Data
Calkins, Lucy McCormick.
  A quick guide to teaching second-grade writers with units of study / Lucy Calkins.
      p. cm. — (Workshop help desk series)
  Includes bibliographical references.
  ISBN 13: 978-0-325-02677-0
  ISBN 10: 0-325-02677-7
  1. English language—Composition and exercises—Study and teaching (Primary).
2. Second grade (education). I. Title. II. Series.
  LB1528.C355 2009
  372.62′3–dc22   2008050386

SERIES EDITOR: *Lucy Calkins and the Teachers College Reading and Writing Project*
EDITOR: *Kate Montgomery*
DEVELOPMENT EDITOR: *Kathy Collins*
PRODUCTION: *Elizabeth Valway*
COVER DESIGN: *Jenny Jensen Greenleaf*
COVER PHOTO: *Peter Cunningham*
INTERIOR DESIGN: *Jenny Jensen Greenleaf*
COMPOSITION: *House of Equations, Inc.*
MANUFACTURING: *Steve Bernier*

Printed in the United States of America on acid-free paper
13 12 11 VP 3 4 5

*For Julia Mooney,
with thanks for her brilliance
and dedication.*

CONTENTS

INTRODUCTION

Second-grade teachers face special challenges in the teaching of writing. Howard Gardner describes second graders as youngsters entering into "the age of competence," suggesting this is the time when children need to develop the competence and confidence to weather the self-critical self-consciousness that comes with adolescence. Of course, in many school systems, standardized tests rain down on children as early as third grade and much of the curriculum is geared toward these tests, so second grade is often the last reprieve for kids. It's a window of time in which children can grow in leaps and bounds—if only those of us around them urge them on!

A class of second graders is an especially diverse group—there will be some who are still fledgling writers and some who are ready for anything you put before them. Your teaching will need to be assessment based and designed to support diversity. Becoming familiar with curriculum developed for first and third graders will help you find different ways to support both your struggling and your strongest writers. The *Units of Study for Primary Writing* (Calkins et al. 2003) and the *Units of Study for Teaching Writing, Grades 3–5* (Calkins et al. 2006) can be helpful resources.

Second-grade teachers also comprise a diverse group. Some of you teach in a school that works directly with the

Teachers College Reading and Writing Project (TCRWP). Others are part of a group of teachers in a building or district that has been studying and using the primary *Units of Study* set. And then there are those of you for whom this is an introduction to writing workshop, who have turned to this because you are seeking an alternative to your existent writing curriculum. Whichever position you hold, we welcome you.

Special Advice for Second-Grade Teachers

No matter what your experience is as a teacher of writing or what your students' writing proficiency may be, if I had to specify how any second-grade teacher might lift the level of her students' writing, I would make the following suggestions.

First, a high *volume* of writing is incredibly important. When children arrive in your classroom at the start of second grade, ideally they will be able to write at least a couple of sentences per page across all the pages in three- to five-page booklets—and produce roughly that quantity of writing during a typical day's writing workshop, although we acknowledge there will be a range of abilities with regard to volume. By third grade, your children will be expected to write at least one notebook page of writing during one day's writing workshop. Your goal by the end of this year will be that children will produce close to a page of writing in one day's writing workshop. To support this goal, it is important to imbue writing time with high expectations, to commit to at least forty minutes of actual pen-to-paper writing time each day, and to provide paper that contains more lines and booklets that contain more pages as the year goes on.

Second, as second graders create more volume of writing, encourage them to *revise, rethink, and rewrite* in order to lift the level of their writing. The challenge is to help children write more without sacrificing clarity, craft, or their readers' interest. This means teaching qualities of good writing, starting with the most fundamental ones including structure, focus, and detail, and it means teaching children that revision is an everyday part of all writing. When you confer, encourage writers to aim not just to record their ideas but also to write well, and help them learn to reread and revise their writing. As the year progresses, revision will also sometimes involve a sequence of drafts.

Third, it is important that children work with increasing *independence*. In your minilessons, you will often remind writers of the options they have to draw upon during that day's writing workshop. As you confer, much of the instruction will not match the minilesson. That is, you'll offer children an assortment of options during minilessons, conferences, and small-group work, so that at any given time in the day what one child does may well differ from what another child does. When you allow your children to take ownership of the choices they make as they write, you are following the essential principles and beliefs that inform writing workshop.

An Overview of the Year

My colleagues at the Teachers College Reading and Writing Project and scores of skilled second-grade teachers contributed to the thinking that underlies this book and the curricular pathway that the book sets forth.

We recommend starting the year with two consecutive units on personal narrative writing, with the second aimed toward lifting the level of writing. We suggest following this with a unit on fiction writing. Before the winter holiday, we hope you have time for a unit on writing fairy tales.

We then move into a January unit on idea-based writing. We imagine that Writing to Grow Ideas will be a unit that will help students write to learn and, especially, write about ideas, including ideas related to their personal narrative writing, to stuff in the world, and to books. Students then bridge into an ambitious unit, a variation on All-About Books. We call this a unit on Expert Books. This unit will incorporate some of the writing-about-ideas and writing-to-learn work that children will have done during the previous month.

After March, we hope you help your children continue down their path of nonnarrative writing by exploring avenues of persuasive writing, specifically review writing—TV show reviews, restaurant reviews, book reviews. This way, students are writing about reading in units, in sequence: Writing to Grow Ideas, Expert Books, and Persuasive Writing.

April is reserved for poetry. May revisits Expert Books, this time inviting children to write expert projects in a content area (we envision this occurring in a science unit, although of course you can choose any topic you like). Finally, we imagine that June will feature a unit angled toward large-scale revision, inviting children to revise narratives they wrote *earlier* in the year. You'll invite children to self-assess their writing and help them make one final push to lift the level of their narrative writing so they are ready for third grade. Some of the narratives they write during this final month could become part of their rite of passage to third grade, traveling with them from one classroom, one grade, one year, to another.

September	Narrative Writing—Revisiting and Re-energizing Small Moments
October	Raising the Level of Narrative Writing with Authors as Mentors
November	Writing and Revising Realistic Fiction
December	The World of Wonder: Fairy Tale Adaptations and Original Fantasy Stories
January	Writing to Grow Ideas (Including Ideas About Books)
February	Expert Projects: Writing to Learn and to Teach About a Topic of Personal Expertise
March	Persuasive Writing: Persuasive Letters and Reviews
April	Poetry
May	Expert Projects in a Content Area: Writing to Learn and to Teach About Science
June	Revision and Assessment

You'll find that I describe the first five months of second grade in detail and then only shine a spotlight down the path of the remaining months. By February, I will have helped you teach your youngsters all the essentials of narrative and non-narrative writing, and I believe you'll be able to coconstruct the remaining units.

A QUICK GUIDE TO

Teaching Second-Grade Writers
with Units of Study

Narrative Writing— Revisiting and Re-energizing Small Moments

W e suggest beginning the year by launching a unit of study on personal narrative writing—a unit I refer to as Small Moments. By definition, personal narratives are stories about one's life written chronologically. They contain characters; the main character is the author of the piece; and they take place in a setting. There is a plot with a couple of events occurring in the period of time in the story, and there tends to be a problem that is solved, a tension that is resolved, or a change that occurs (see "Small Moments" in *Units of Study for Primary Writing* [Calkins et al. 2003]).

There are several reasons to begin the year with narrative writing. When a child reads a story, the child uses words to create a virtual experience. Writing stories is the reciprocal process to reading stories; in both instances, children rely on words to create and operate within the alternate world of another time and place. Human beings come to know each other through the sharing of stories, and beginning the year with a personal narrative unit provides opportunities to build community. Then, too, narrative writing is an essential component of most other kinds of writing—even persuasive letter writing includes writing anecdotes (which are really Small Moment stories). More than this, your children will be reading lots of narrative texts; the more they understand how those texts are made, the more they can construct meaning as they read and write.

Assessing Writers at the Start of the Year

Although you may be eager to get writing workshop under way, it's important to take time to assess your writers and collect baseline data right away. We suggest devoting one day's writing workshop to assessment. You might say, "Before we get started, I would love to see what you can do as writers of true stories. Today, I'm going to give you a booklet that you'll use to draw and then write a story on one particular thing that you did. Make this an example of the best true-story writing you can do. I'm not going to be helping you today—instead I'll be working away on my own story!"

Teachers often provide forty minutes of actual writing time and refrain from giving any reminders or assistance. We recommend using writing booklets that contain plenty of pages (five, perhaps) and plenty of lines on each page (more than five). Tell children they can add more pages if necessary. If you sit down and actually write on that day, it is important to do so without huge fanfare so that your children don't use your writing as a model. You want to see what they can do all on their own. Resist the temptation to nudge kids to revise a piece of writing or to scaffold children to do work that is far beyond what they will be able to soon do on their own.

Once the writing time is over, make sure that each booklet contains the child's name and the date, and then look at these pieces alongside a narrative continuum that shows the developmental stages of writing and names the qualities of writing that define each stage. You needn't match every single trait; just look between the piece that the child has written and the sample pieces of writing for each level and do the best you can to locate the child's on-demand writing within the scale. You'll be able to look ahead on the continuum to see the work you'll encourage him to do over the next few months and to see specific techniques that you can complement and teach.

After two months of work in narrative writing, you'll redo this assessment, saying exactly the same things and providing the same conditions, and then watching to see how much your children have grown in that time. You may use both September and the late-October writing at your parent-teacher conferences to discuss children's growth.

Getting Started on Writing Small Moment Narratives

After the one-day assessment, you'll be ready to begin the Small Moments unit. If your students are new to this curriculum, it will be easy to inspire them by saying, "Writers, this year you are going to write the important moments from your life. We are going to call these pieces *Small Moment stories*." If you demonstrate with your own writing and share a couple of stories written by children—making sure the children's work represents a range of developmental levels—your youngsters will be ready to start writing.

If your students wrote Small Moment stories the year before, your challenge this year is to generate excitement about once again writing Small Moment stories, and so you'll want to convey that there will be new layers of difficulty in this year's work. You'll need to decide on how to accomplish this goal.

For example, at the end of the school year, perhaps the first-grade teachers told children to save artifacts of their first-grade writing lives in a time capsule. If first graders saved one of their best Small Moment stories from first grade, then when these youngsters cross the threshold into second grade, they can retrieve the saved treasures and recall their old writing lives. The first writing project for those children could then be to reread and rethink those earlier stories, making them even better. This, of course, would provide a physical, hands-on way for children and for their new teachers, too, to recall what children have already learned to do, building on that foundation at the start of second grade.

You need not start the year that way. You could come up with other ways to create a drumroll around the idea that children will be writing Small Moment stories. As you read the description of this month, you can select any goal to spotlight so that you can say, "Like last year, you'll write Small Moment stories. You already learned that writers do *x, y,* and *z*. This year, you'll again have the chance to do all of that, but this year, you are in *second grade*, so you're *also* going to . . ." For example, you could emphasize that this year, the moments they select to write about will be both small *and big* ones. Learning to imbue a story with significance is gigantic work and this will certainly be one aspect of narrative craft that you teach this year. Another option is to tell children at the start of the year that this year, they'll not only be writing Small Moment stories but storytelling them as well, and writing with the voices of storytellers. One way or another, you'll rally kids to not only recall all that they have already learned but also work with zeal toward ambitious new goals.

As I mentioned earlier, there are a few things that are especially essential for this year, one of which is stamina. The secret to stamina lies in the paper that you give to your children. Start the year by providing kids with booklets, not single pages, on which to write—and those booklets can each contain five pages, with each page containing only a very small box for the picture and plenty of lines for the writing. It is impossible to overemphasize the power that the paper itself has for conveying expectations. As children become more skilled as writers, steer them toward paper with more lines, encouraging them to write more, and from the start, be sure you differentiate by giving paper with more lines to children who are ready for it.

Generating Story Ideas

Early in the unit, remind children that they can come up with ideas for true stories easily by simply thinking of things that they have done. They can think about what they did over the summer, the weekend, the previous day. They can think about what happened that morning at home, on the way to school, on the playground, while coming in to school. One thing we've learned is that children's writing will be much more powerful if they decide to write about experiences that matter to them, moments that are both small and big, rather than try to write to a specific sort of prompt.

One way to guide children toward writing about moments that are personally significant is to encourage them to write about something that happened that gave them a strong feeling—something that was really funny or really scary or really sad or really joyful. You could also teach children that sometimes writers think about things that have happened to us that we want to tell others about. You might suggest that writers sometimes think about particular small moments when the writer was the hero—a particular time when the writer helped someone, or taught someone, or accomplished something, or learned something. You could add, "Lots of times others probably didn't notice these tiny moments of heroism, but you know the moment was a special one." It's important that you and the students understand that these are suggestions but the choice of which strategy to use is up to each child. Soon children will be drawing from a list of several optional strategies for coming up with true stories and for making sure their Small Moments are both small *and* big.

A word of caution: We recommend spending no more than a few days teaching several strategies to generate story ideas. We don't want students to think the purpose of a mini-lesson is for the teacher to lay out a new strategy for generating ideas that they will then use that day. In other words, we don't want the class to become dependent on us to jump-start their writing every day. Instead, we want them to become accustomed to writing every day and knowing that life itself gives them story ideas. All this is to say that after just two or three days of demonstrating strategies for generating writing ideas, you should shift your teaching toward helping children write those story ideas.

Teaching a Crucial Characteristic of Effective Narrative Writing

The single most important skill to teach writers of stories is a skill that is sometimes referred to as *show, don't tell*. Often people misunderstand this term, thinking that it means simply that a writer should show a character is feeling something (e.g., "He clenched his fists and stomped away.") rather than say it (e.g., "He was mad."). Actually, the advice to show rather than to tell is much more profound than that. In order to storytell well, a writer needs to do what a reader does when reading a story. The writer needs to put herself in the shoes of the main character and re-create, in her mind, the evolving drama of that time and place.

So if I am going to write about taking my son to college and helping him fix up his room, I can't stand outside that event and talk about it, or I will be summarizing, not story-telling. I'll be summarizing if I say, "I remember when John and I took Evan to college. It was really hard. I wanted to set up his room perfectly." Instead, I need to begin by asking myself, "What will be the starting point of the story?" If the starting point is the moment when we stopped the car outside Evan's dorm room, I need to go back in my mind to just before that moment and start reliving it so I can write it in a storytelling manner. I might write, "'There's a space right by the door,' I said, pointing. John pulled the car to a stop alongside Evan's dorm. I opened the door and got out, turning back to collect an armload of suitcases. . . ."

It is a challenge to help seven-year-olds ask themselves, "When in the sequence of events will my story start?" and for them to reimagine (or relive) the experience, capturing it bit by bit onto the page. There are a number of potential hard parts. One, certainly, is for the writer to realize that a story about catching a fish need not begin with waking up or with catching the fish. Instead, it can begin with threading the worm onto the hook, or with casting, or with arriving at the stream. There are options, and generally the best place to start is just a bit before the heart of the story.

Another challenge is for the writer to relive or re-create the event. When a child says, "I can't remember what I did!" it is important to respond, "Imagine what you *probably* did and said." Of course, children can imagine in sweeping steps ("I caught a fish.") or in great detail ("I settled down on a log that I'd made into a chair and tried to hold the fishing rod very still."). What can we say or do to help children write more like the latter than the former? That's a mystery for all teachers of writing, but chances are that one important step is to listen to children in ways that help them know the details of their lives matter. So when they are sharing a story from their lives, we can listen closely and ask things such as, "So what was that like?" "What were you thinking right then?" "Help me picture that," or "Can you say more about that?"

Rehearsing for Writing

You'll want to teach your children that writers take time to rehearse their writing. In other words, they do not simply pick up a pen and start writing their narratives, because when they do that, their narratives read more like summaries. Instead, writers take time to rehearse. We suggest taking a firm stance about the importance of rehearsal and teaching strategies for rehearsing that will lead your students away from summaries and toward stories.

In first grade, perhaps your students learned to touch each page in a story booklet, saying aloud the exact words that they planned to eventually write on that page. This method for rehearsal is enormously powerful and useful. Another strategy for rehearsal is to teach your second graders to storytell multiple times before drafting a story. Teach them to think, "How do I want listeners to feel?" and then tell their story in a way so that readers really feel that. Say, "Think, 'What is the good part of this story?' and this time, tell it so that you really build up the good part."

Once children have said aloud the exact words they might write for one page, the next, and the next, then they can begin writing. However, children sometimes tend to run the whole story together, writing not only about starting sledding but about sledding itself all on one page. When this happens, it helps to teach writers they can jot a subtitle or sketch an icon or quick picture onto each page to act as a placeholder to pace the story.

Remember that all your lessons about rehearsing for narrative writing do not need to be taught early in this unit. Children will be cycling through the process of writing many stories. At the very start of the unit, they will all start stories in sync with each other, but soon you will find that one child has finished her first story and is starting on her second while lots of other children are midway through their first stories. This means that during the second, third, and fourth weeks of this unit, you'll still be able to teach children strategies for rehearsing for writing. Always, your teaching will remind children of the repertoire of strategies they already have access to and will help them know yet another strategy or another way to use the strategies.

Supporting Your Children as They Cycle Through the Writing Process

Within this one unit, you can expect that second graders will write approximately six or seven five-page-long stories with perhaps approximately five or six sentences on a page. Those are rough estimates and certainly many children can do more than this, especially when we hold high, yet realistic, expectations that second graders can write more than a page a day and much more than one book a month. Many teachers have found that it's quite reasonable to expect that a child will rehearse for and write a story in approximately two or three days, revising it a bit while writing the draft, especially if the teacher reaches the child in time to support this, and revising it more extensively on the next day. Expect that at this time of the year, those revisions will be written right onto the original draft and will probably not yield a whole new draft. Then the child will get started on another story.

Typically if the whole class begins writing a story on day one, a third of the students will probably have gone as far as they can go without teacher input by early in day three, another third will have received support from the teacher and will be revising so as to continue working till the start of day four, and some children won't be ready to start their next piece until the start of day five. This means that the class will not progress through the writing process is sync with each other (although by day five of your first week, you might announce a deadline to push along kids who need a nudge).

As children move through rehearsal, drafting, and revision, your teaching, too, should cycle between these processes. You can't devote the first third of the month to rehearsal work as if children are writing just one piece and will rehearse it for ten days before progressing to drafting. Instead, your teaching will shift from strategies that pertain to rehearsal, to those that pertain to drafting, to those that pertain to revision along with the bulk of your class, which means that you'll devote just a day or sometimes two to each of these before moving to the next process. Imagine, then, that you'll teach rehearsal strategies on something like days one, two, five, nine, and thirteen of the unit and drafting strategies on days three, six, ten, and fourteen of the unit.

This also means that if you teach a concept halfway through this first unit—perhaps teaching children that when characters talk, it helps if they usually use direct address, complete with quotations—then a child could conceivably use the new strategy across the stories in her writing folder. For example, on the day of your lesson on writing with direct address, you may ask children to reread all the stories they have written thus far in the year (perhaps with a partner), looking for instances in which the text summarizes rather than uses direct address. If one child spots a page that says, "My mom told me she was going to go," the child might revise this so the page now reads, "My mom said, 'I'm going.'"

Once a child has written several stories, he can use classroom charts as a scaffold and can go back on his own initiative to revise for any of the concepts you have taught thus far in the unit. Support this sort of independence and initiative because independence is an important goal in a writing workshop.

Each day during the writing workshop, writers will work on their writing, and in order to do so, they will draw on their full, composite repertoire of strategies. That is, your children should know how to come up with story ideas, get started, write, finish, reread, revise, and get started on another story all without needing teacher involvement. This will allow them to cycle through the writing process with independence, leaving you free enough to teach writing rather than manage their writing process during conferences.

While your children cycle through the process, writing up a storm, notice their command of the conventions of written language. Some children will come into your class writing their drafts without a lot of concern for spelling, not pausing for even a second to spell even the words they almost know by heart, and others will obsess over every word and want your seal of approval for every decision. Differentiate your instruction, helping the fast-and-free writers take that extra second to remember to write in lowercase letters (unless uppercase letters are required) and spell words they almost know by heart as correctly as they can while still writing quickly. That is, you are definitely not expecting perfect spelling, but you are expecting children to write an increasing number of words correctly with ease and automaticity. You'll also want your fast-and-free writers to become increasingly accustomed to inserting end punctuation into their texts as they write. Meanwhile, help the children who see writing as little more than an exercise on spelling and penmanship focus much more on writing quickly, fluently, and with a focus on content.

One way to support children in cycling through the writing process at their own speeds is by setting up partnerships. By the third day of school, each writer can sit beside a partner in the meeting area and also meet with that person during many mid-workshop interruptions and share sessions. You do not need to know your children well before you link them into these short-term partnerships. You also need to be willing for children to write as best they can, revise as best they can, edit as best they can, and then move to another piece—all without necessarily getting a green light from you. Remember that their drafts will all accumulate in a folder, and toward the end of the unit, you will ask children to select their best to revise and edit more extensively, so at that point you can catch up to kids who never did all the refinements you'd love for them to do!

In order for your children to progress through the writing process with some independence, channel some of your teaching time toward the goal of establishing a productive community within the classroom. It will be much easier to induct children into the norms of a writing workshop if they were part of a similar workshop the year before, but either way, remember that you need to explicitly teach children your expectations for how they'll act during writing. Remind children how to convene in and disperse from the meeting area. Act this out yourself, physically showing kids how to push in chairs, come swiftly to the meeting area, sit cross-legged on top of their writing folder in their assigned rug spot, and reread the charts that hang near the meeting area. Similarly, explicitly teach children what you want them to do when you pause in the midst of a minilesson to say, "Turn and talk," or "Stop and jot." Whether children have been working in this manner for a year or two now, or are brand new to this way of workshop, you can expect them to learn to turn on a dime to talk with a partner, and you can also expect them to attend to your signal that time for talking or jotting is over.

Important Content You Can Teach Throughout the Writing Process

Once your children are all cycling though the writing process and drawing on their cumulative repertoire of strategies and their growing knowledge of good writing, you'll be free to teach in ways that lift the level of their writing. Draw upon knowledge of content that is apt to especially pay off for second-grade writers.

First of all, one of the most important things you can do to lift the level of children's stories is to help them write stories that are long and fully developed, yet also focused. For many children, those two goals are contradictions. They are all set to write long stories with lots of words, thereby impressing you and others with their new powers of spelling and handwriting, but the drawback is often that their long stories are unfocused. The stories wind up telling one thing after another after another after another. If you are going to teach children to write stories that are both long *and* focused, it is really important that *you* grasp how to do this. Sometimes kids get confused because, in fact, teachers are confused. For starters, think about focus this way: for second graders, writing personal narratives that are focused generally means the stories will chronicle events that lasted around twenty minutes.

Also teach children that after they finish writing a story, they can reread it and think about ways they can fix it up. "The Craft of Revision," from *Units of Study for Primary Writing* (Calkins et al. 2003), provides additional ideas for minilessons to teach during this portion of your unit. The most important lesson on revision might be this: writers need to become *readers*, and we need to read our writing as if we have never read it before, asking especially, "Does this make sense? Is this clear?" Writers revise to make sure our writing is clear and sensible.

You'll also want to encourage children to think of their drafts as physically malleable. A good place to begin is to have children try out different ways to start or end a story, attaching flaps onto their paper, with each flap containing another draft of a lead or an ending. Children can also revise to make characters talk—including the exact words each character said. They can reread to identify and then embellish especially important parts of the story, adding onto these sections of the story. Of course, many children may have learned these strategies last year, but chances are they will have forgotten to do all these things. Don't take four months to remind them of what they have already learned!

Then, too, throughout this month, you can continue to coach children to make even their first drafts a bit more conventionally correct. Remind your students that writers think of a sentence of thought, write that thought down in a rush, then add the period. Then the writer thinks of the next thought, and begins to write it using a capital letter for the first word, and again writes in a rush, ending that sentence with another period. That is, punctuation is not an afterthought to be inserted during editing!

The Finishing Touch: Selecting the Best Piece to Revise for an Audience

At the end of the unit, children will choose their best work and revise this more deeply and extensively, with help from you. One of the best, most exciting ways for children to revise narratives is by using drama to see what they have said and what they might say next. A writer and his partner could read a bit of the writer's text aloud, then act out that bit and then read the next bit and act it out. The actors will quickly realize things that have been left out. "No, you need to do this!" they'll say, and then the obvious comment, "You should say that in the story!" Imagining their narratives as the basis for little plays can help children understand the fundamental concept behind narrative writing.

There are other ways to revise as well. Children could rewrite the most important page in their story, taking smaller steps through the progression of events and thoughts on that one page. This revision process can last for a few days, and it can, if you'd like, involve taping flaps of paper onto the bottom or the sides of a draft, using staple removers to open books up so that one page can be removed and a new one substituted, and so forth.

After children revise their selected work, they will need to edit it. You will presumably already have a word wall featuring a dozen high-frequency words, and if you haven't done so already, teach your children that writers reread, checking to be sure they use word wall words correctly. From now on, after a child writes a draft of any story (even if the writer is not on the verge of publishing it), the writer needs to reread the text, checking that he spelled the word wall words correctly.

After your second graders fix some spellings and add some punctuation to their stories, the pieces will probably still be far from correct. You may want to call children into small groups to teach them one more thing—some might benefit from learning about commas, others from learning the spelling of a common word ending. I do not recommend that you then go through the very time-consuming, elaborate process of correcting every error in the child's draft and insisting the child copy that draft over so that it is perfectly conventional. Doing this requires days and days on end, and the work is frankly not very rigorous for kids—they end up just copying your corrections. Meanwhile, the resulting text does not represent what they can do anyhow. These are little kids at the start of the year, and their work will not be perfect. If you intervene to prop the work up so that it matches your high standards, then the work will not represent what your children can do, and later you and others will not be able to look at the progression of published pieces to see ways in which children have grown. Of course, if you or someone else types up the pieces, that person will correct the spellings. But chances are good that if this happens, it will take a number of days before those pieces are all typed. Don't wait for those perfect pieces to be returned to kids before you celebrate the kids' best work and move on to the next unit.

I recommend the simplest possible publishing party so that you get onto the next unit by the start of your second month of school. Perhaps just put writers into small circles and give each child a turn to read aloud, with the listeners chiming in after each author reads. Then gather the kids alongside the bulletin board as each writer leaves his work in the appropriate square, perhaps saying as he does, "I'm proud of the way I . . ."

Raising the Level of Narrative Writing with Authors as Mentors

Instead of rushing children toward a whole new kind of writing, this unit has been designed with the hopes that it will give second graders opportunities to outgrow themselves as writers. For just one more month, they'll continue writing focused personal narratives, but this time touchstone texts and a mentor author will help children aim for higher goals as writers.

The start of the unit will allow you to draw upon "Authors as Mentors," from *Units of Study for Primary Writing* (Calkins et al. 2003). Later in the unit, you'll remind children that their writing, like the published pieces they admire, will be shared with readers; therefore, they will want to write in such a way that readers can read their pieces smoothly and with intonation and feeling. The final portion of this unit can draw upon another book of *Units of Study for Primary Writing*: "Writing for Readers."

During this unit your children will be writing and revising about a half dozen books, each of which will begin as approximately five pages in length (about a paragraph per page) and will become longer through revision. This is not different than the previous unit; the difference is that during this unit, you and your class will look closely at the work of one published writer, letting that writer function as a mentor. One of the most important messages we give to children during a writing workshop is this: "You are writers, like writers the world over." This unit uses that message to lift the quality of children's writing.

The Reading-Writing Connections This Unit Does—and Does Not—Promote

Because writers, and especially young writers, tend to think mostly about the content of their writing, their initial instinct when they study the books that mentor authors have written is to then write books involving the same characters, revolving around similar themes. A child reads Cynthia Rylant's *When I Was Young in the Mountains* (1982) and thinks, "I could write 'When I Was Young in Hamburg, New York.'" In this unit, we hope instead that children continue writing on their own subjects, as they were doing in September. The reading-writing connections that we sponsor involve emulating the *writerly life* and the *craft* rather than the *topics* of mentor texts. They look at how the mentor author lives his or her life to write, and think, "Could I live similarly?" They also look closely at a text (or several texts) in order to notice the author's craftsmanship and think, "What did that author do that I could do as well?"

This unit, then, encourages youngsters to make two kinds of reading-writing connections. First, children imagine the writerly life that the mentor author probably lived, including especially the sort of rehearsal that author probably did, and they try to integrate these strategies into their own writing lives. Then, after children have rehearsed for and drafted their stories, they study the writer's craft in their mentor texts, thinking, "What did this author do that I, too, could try?" and they use those techniques as they revise their stories. At this point in the process, the mentor author helps the apprentice writer refine the style of her draft.

Reading and writing connections are important to this unit, but you also hope children will continue writing personal narratives, drawing on all they have already learned with increasing independence, rehearsing and revising with more gusto and with a new sense of direction. The ultimate goal, then, is for the quality of children's narratives to become dramatically higher.

Teach Children That Writers Live Attentive Lives

Because this unit comes early in the year, we suggest you choose a mentor author who can help children write focused narratives. Some authors and titles to consider are Maribeth Boelts and Noah Jones' *Those Shoes* (2008), Julie Brinkloe's *Fireflies!* (1986), Jonathan London's *Hurricane!* (1998), and Donald Crews' *Shortcut* (1996).

We recommend that you hold off telling your students the name of the whole-class mentor author and text until you have read the book aloud to them, trying to make that experience especially powerful. If the class loves the book, then you can go forward and say, "I can tell that many of you love this text. Let's study what the author has done to write it so well." If nothing magical happens between your class and the text you hope will become a mentor for your class, try another text!

The position we advance in the "Authors as Mentors" book is that you begin this unit by inviting children to live like the writer that they have adopted as a mentor. Suggest that the class as a whole learns about the mentor author so that children can then try to live writerly lives, taking cues from the writer. To help children do this, teach them what you know about the author's life and writing process, stressing what the author has done that you hope children emulate. You might want to locate the author's website and blog, if available, in which the author freely shares the challenges and joys he or she experiences while writing.

For the purpose of this unit, you should emphasize the writerly consciousness that is a unique characteristic of most any author. Even if you do not know much about the life of your particular mentor author, you can let children know that their mentor author, like others, probably pays close attention to the details of life. You can draw on the words *any* writer has written to describe that writerly life. For example, you could read aloud a page or two from *I'm in Charge of Celebrations*, by Byrd Baylor (1995), using that excerpt to show that writers, including your mentor author, don't just walk past all the details of their lives. When a writer drives along a road, she is apt to glance up at the clouds and see that one is shaped like a parrot. Other people might just drive on, but writers say, "My gosh! Look at that!" and pull over.

In "Authors as Mentors," we suggest that in order to live writerly lives, youngsters carry tiny notepads with them, jotting or sketching the little things that happen, and then when it is time to write, they reread those tiny notepads and think, "Could I make one of these ideas into a true story?" If you decide to ask children to carry little notepads with them, purchase the smallest notebooks you can find and then cut them into halves or thirds so that these notepads are truly tiny. Otherwise children start writing their whole stories into these books, and, predictably, those stories end up horribly underdeveloped! You might say to your children, "I bet Donald Crews got the idea for his story *Sail Away* from one day when he sailed and got stuck in a storm. He must have thought to himself, 'I need to remember this moment,' and then jotted or sketched it on a notepad."

You should carry your own Tiny Topics Notepad, too, and make a rather public show out of taking it out to record the small moments that happen in the classroom. "Oh my goodness!" you might say. "I slipped on the ice and Audra kept me from falling. That would make a great story! Let me jot just the words 'slipping on ice—Audra helped' in my Tiny Topics Notepad to hold onto that idea." Show students how to take brief notes and use those notes to help them remember a moment.

Remind Children to Draw on What They Already Learned About Rehearsal

Once a child has selected a moment to write in detail, that child needs to rehearse the story with a partner. Your children will have already learned strategies for rehearsing stories during the previous unit, so act surprised if they do not automatically draw on those strategies and refer to those charts. For example, during the first unit, children learned to touch the pages of their booklets (and perhaps to quickly sketch the sequence of microevents) and then to storytell each bit of the story, stretching out each part of it. Expect your second graders to do this without your nudging now. When children storytell, coach them to elaborate without letting the story lose its focus. The story about slipping on the ice, for example, might be told (and hopefully written) like this: "One sunny winter day, I was walking to the park in my new brown boots. They were shiny. All of a sudden, I slipped on a patch of ice. My feet came out from under me and I almost went down on my butt. Then I felt a hand on my arm. It was Audra coming to save me. We laughed. Then . . . my feet started to slip again. . . ."

A Spiral Curriculum for Teaching Children to Study and Emulate Craftsmanship

After two or three days in which children have lived like authors, collecting moments in Tiny Topics Notepads and then writing these as stories across the pages in booklets, tell your students that writers often study the work of a mentor author to see *how* that author made his or her story into a wonderful one. Teach them to do this not by scanning the text looking for bits that illustrate qualities of good writing the children have already learned, but instead by letting the text itself lead them to think in new ways about qualities of good writing. Ask them to first simply note a place or two in the text that really got to them, a place that is especially powerful, and then to think, "What did the author do that I could try?" In London's (1998) picture book about the onset of a hurricane, for example, there is a page when the action really picks up, and children might select that page as especially powerful. If they examine what exactly London did in order to make this page read differently, the children might notice that the page contains dialogue. It is, in fact, not just any ol' dialogue. The passages of talk ring true and sound real. Listen to Mom: "A hurricane!" "It's coming our way!" "Hurry up." "Pack quickly!" Those sentences all sound like they could have been said in the moment of the story. The children, however, may or may not notice what it is about the dialogue that makes it effective.

Once you and the children have noticed that an author uses a technique such as making characters talk (perhaps in ways that ring true to that moment of time), return to a text that you worked on publicly earlier in the year—your own story or a whole-class story—and then invite children to help you reread, thinking about whether there are places you could have used this technique for good purpose. Of course, you'll want to have eyed the situation ahead of time and found that, yes, the technique you spotlight in the mentor text *is* one that could lift the level of your writing. You can then rewrite one section of your writing using the new technique, and the children can try this with another section (leave the passage in your text that can most easily be improved for the kids). Then, invite children to reread their own writing in a similar way, checking to see if the technique is also one that could lift the level of their writing. Any one technique may not be applicable to every piece of writing, so the author's technique itself is not the big idea here. Instead, the more important lesson is that children can find any number of techniques that a mentor author uses and then go back to find places in their own writing where they could use that same technique to good effect.

At first, children will summarize a craft move with just a word or a phrase: "The characters talked" or "He put in feelings." This is what you should expect at the very start of this unit, and for the time being, continue on with the major progression of activities that I describe in this chapter. For example, if your second graders notice that the character talked, accept this way of naming what works in a text—after all, this is a terrifically important craft technique—then encourage them to notice other examples of this same technique in the mentor text, and then to emulate this technique in their own writing, too. They'll all have lots of success doing this, and you will have launched the new work of this unit and hopefully gotten all your children feeling they can do what you are teaching and can even work with some independence. In this instance, your children's cycle of writing should now involve living writerly lives, noticing small moments, choosing one of these to write as a story, rehearsing by sketching and storytelling across five or so pages, writing the story, then studying a mentor author, noticing what that mentor author has done, then emulating that technique as a way to revise the child's draft, then moving on to find yet another small moment and to rehearse that second small moment, and so on.

Early in the unit, allow this work to proceed at a relatively low level, making sure all children can participate in the gist of making reading-writing connections, doing so as they continue drafting and revising their Small Moment narratives. Some of your teaching during this section of the unit will revolve around helping children draw from all they learned earlier in the year. You'll probably have to remind writers how to include punctuation as they write, generating sentences of thought, punctuating on the run. Punctuation should not be an afterthought that writers insert once a text is completed, although of course once a text is completed, writers can reread, using punctuation as road signs, finding places where the punctuation may need to be altered.

You will also need to give children practical lessons in revision. You might have to remind them they can rewrite a page of a book, stapling a new draft of that page on top of the old draft. They can also tuck more words into a passage, using carets. Help them see their initial draft as malleable.

As children continue cycling through the writing process, producing more Small Moment stories, intervene in ways that lift the level of the reading-writing connections they are making and that help them think in increasingly powerful ways about qualities of good writing. As always, you should alter the sophistication of your teaching so that you are within your children's zone of proximal development (Vygotsky 1978). You may decide that some of what I suggest in this chapter is out of range for many of your children, and you could use this only within small-group instruction with some of your stronger writers. Alternatively, you could teach a second unit later in the school year on authors as mentors and use some of this at that time. That is, a teacher always needs to teach in response to one's own students, and this means adjusting the level of your teaching so that you march just a bit ahead of your children.

You will want to help children talk with much more specificity about what, *exactly*, made this particular technique so effective. Point out the decisions the author made, the path he could have—but didn't—take. "He *could* have just said, 'I felt sad,' but he didn't, did he? Instead he wrote x. What, exactly, do you think he did here that makes this part convey feelings in such a powerful way? What makes this particular detail, description, or bit of dialogue so effective?"

Although at first you should allow children to talk about qualities of good writing as if it were true that good writing "includes talk" or "has feelings," the truth is that a text can include talk and feelings and be horrible, or it can do this and be effective. The challenge is to include talk (or feelings) in ways that are effective—and this is not easy to teach or to talk about.

If you nudge children to be more specific about what works in a text, they will probably spout off the terms that you have taught them: "He showed, not told, his feelings." "He used details." Of course you always want to celebrate times when your teaching has an impact on your children. On the other hand, you also want to extend what your children are doing, and one way to do this is to help them open up any of these pat phrases. For starters, it is transformational if you simply get children using more words to specify what exactly the author did. Generally, talking about what works in a text requires a sentence or two, not a word. Although at first you will demonstrate what you mean by talking long about a bit of craftsmanship, the goal is for your children to reach for ways to articulate what they notice about an author's craft.

It's important to note that there is no one correct way to name what an author has done in a text. One passage can illustrate a variety of writerly techniques. For example, a bit of dialogue could be heralded as an example of an author making his characters talk by writing the exact words they say or that same passage could show that the author changes how a character talks to show the character's changing feelings.

Chances are good that both you and your children will find it challenging to learn to talk well about qualities of good writing in these ways. There are a few crucial tips that can help. For one thing, once you have identified a passage that works, think about how the author could have written that same passage differently, in ways that wouldn't work. When the hurricane was approaching, instead of talking in short sentences, the mother could have used long ones, saying, "It seems likely to me that this would be a good time to run." Then ask, "If this section had been written in that different way, why would it have been less effective?" That process often leads you to a conclusion—"It helps to use language that sounds and feels true to the moment."

In addition to teaching children to ask themselves, "How would this text have been different if the mentor author had written this differently?" teach them that after they notice one place in the text where the author has used a particular craft technique, it helps to see if the author used that same technique in other places. Before any of us can see several instances of a craftsmanship technique, the words used to describe that craft technique often need to be reworded so they are transferable from one passage to another; the important thing about this generalization is that it also means those words will be more helpful to writers as they turn toward their own drafts. By finding several examples of a craft technique, students learn that the same technique can be used in different ways, in different places, and this increases the possibility of students transferring the technique to their own writing.

Although a child can work individually to name what an author has done that works, many children in a classroom can also work together to talk about what they see in a text and what the author seems to have done to create this effect. Out of these shared conversations, the class will develop its own *metalanguage*. The work of developing a language for talking and thinking about texts is far more important than having young children incorporate proper literary terms into this language. There will certainly be times, however, when you'll decide to tell children that there are specific words in the world that people use to describe certain craft moves. That is, after a week or two of talking about how the author uses "dot dot dot," you might say, "Guys, I realized the other day that grown-ups notice the same thing we notice, only instead of talking about *dot dot dot*, they talk about *ellipses*."

These craft techniques can be collected onto a craft chart that the students can use to remind them of all that you have taught. The chart might, in the end, include techniques such as building suspense, using sensory images, using comparisons, using repetition, using sound words, and writing in small actions to slow down the story. Ask the students to agree upon a class name for each technique. For each craft move, the chart can include an example or two of instances when the technique has been used and also note the effect the technique has had on readers. There are examples of this type of chart in "Authors as Mentors," from *Units of Study for Primary Writing* (Calkins et al. 2003), and in Katie Wood Ray's book *Wondrous Words* (1999).

The craft chart and all your teaching can help children work with independence. That is, after the first day or two, be very careful that you don't set up an atmosphere in which all children try out the same technique at one time. The idea is not for children to be working in sync. Rather, kids should be generating their own ideas and using those ideas in their own writing. The goal is that children try techniques that resonate for them—ones they admire—and that they draw on a mentor author's craft moves as they make their own. What works for one child's writing won't necessarily work for another's.

As your students progress in this unit, be sure to remind them that when they want to try an author's technique, they'll need to use all the revision tools that you have available in the room. Revision needs to be an effortless part of writing for these kids, and not just what a writer does in preparation for publication. Keep the revision tools on hand—swatches of paper for additions, scissors and tape, staple removers and staplers.

A tip about structure: As kids learn to write focused personal narratives, we often stress the importance that Small

Moment stories always involve just one single moment. As your children gain control over writing Small Moment stories, teach them that, in fact, most focused narratives require two vignettes, or two scenes (as in scenes in a play), in order to unroll the story. That is, in a story about getting a bike, the writer may first tell about the day his best friend got a bike and rode off, leaving him standing forlorn alongside the road. Then the text can jump ahead to the big moment when the author's family sings "Happy Birthday" and his dad struggles into the room with a giant box, out of which comes a bike, which the author then wheels out onto the road and climbs aboard. Notice in this little story that the plot involves what could be described as two small moments (or two vignettes), one representing the beginning and one telling what happened later (or the middle and the end). Notice, too, that the small moments are not sixty seconds long, as some children seem to believe!

Writing for Readers

During the final week of this unit of study, you may want to remind children that they are writing literature and tell them that when a book is really well written, it can become a perfect book for reading aloud. But such books need to sound right to the ear. This can lead you to help children reread and revise and edit a selected text or two, making sure that those texts are powerful enough to join others in the read-aloud basket.

You could suggest that for the next few days, each child take a book that she has decided would be a good read-aloud text and revise that book to make it into the best read-aloud text possible. As part of this work, you'll also want to channel children to care about their conventions so that readers can read their texts smoothly. Ask children to exchange papers with a partner and to listen as the partner reads the writer's text aloud. What causes the partner to stumble? Those are sections that merit more work, and not only from the child but also from you. It may be that many of your students are not yet writing with end-of-sentence punctuation, or that many of them are not even spelling very common high-frequency words correctly—words like *said* and *have* and *then*. There may be students in your class who still sprinkle capital letters hither and yon throughout their writing. Some writers may still be recording only some of the sounds they hear in a word rather than relying on the look of words and on words they know how to spell. If these descriptors match most of your second graders, then your emphasis in minilessons during this final portion of the unit will be on some of these essential conventions of written language. Teach children to write with periods, to use capital letters only when they are warranted, to take the time to spell word wall words correctly, to draw on the spellings they know in order to invent spellings they do not know, and so on. You may also decide that you need to look again at your work with spelling and phonics, work that presumably happens in another section of your day, to make sure that that work is developmentally appropriate— one size does not fit all when it comes to phonics and spelling.

Once partners have finished reading each other's pieces aloud looking for parts that are difficult to read and working on bottom-line conventions, suggest partners reconvene to think about which passages should be read in which way (based on meaning) and then to work together to provide punctuation road signs and to vary sentences. This way, other readers will read the text with feeling. "This is the sad part," the writer might say to a partner. "Read this like you are really sad." Then two partnerships can exchange papers and listen to how others read their texts, diving back into those texts to alter them. As part of this process, you can help writers reach for techniques such as alliteration, parallelism, repetition, and onomatopoeia, which can all make a text sound better.

But you will especially want to teach children that writers can use punctuation (and the complex sentence structures that generally accompany varied punctuation) to guide readers to vary their intonation. Many of your second graders will write sentences that have many "and then . . . and then . . . and then . . ." sentences that go on endlessly. Show children how to add subordinate phrases to their sentences. In *Owl Moon*, for example, Yolen (1987) could have written, "Pa and I went owling. We went owling at night. It was past my bedtime." Instead she combines a lot of information into a sentence that tells not only what she did but when she did it and under what conditions she did it. "Late last night, long past my bedtime, Pa and I went owling." Children can try similar work. Instead of writing, "I went to the park," a child can write, "Early Saturday morning, just after breakfast, I went to the park." Students can also learn to tuck in more information about the main people, places, and things they write about. A child could write, "I went to the park, the one down the street from me," or "I went to the park, where I saw rows and rows of swings and a giant slide."

Draw on or adapt whichever minilessons seem appropriate to your kids from the *Units of Study for Primary Writing* (Calkins et al. 2003) unit "Writing for Readers." You can use abbreviated versions of some of these minilessons to support small-group work. We envision that all but sessions two, five, nine, and twelve could be adaptable as either minilessons, mid-workshop teaching points, or the teaching kernel in a teaching share. At this point in the school year, we suggest you give kids a second on-demand writing assessment, paying attention to how they've grown from the one you gave at the very start of the year.

Plan a Culminating Celebration

When the month draws to a close, celebrate your students' growth as writers by having them publish their books as picture books that resemble those of their mentor authors. They can study how these authors created titles for their books and wrote dedications and "About the Author" sections. Authors also have publication parties where they share snippets of their books with an audience. You will definitely want to place your children's published books in your classroom library, or on a special shelf in your library, making them available as read-aloud texts (and options during independent reading).

Writing and Revising Realistic Fiction

I t's likely that your students will be very excited to write fiction! November is a perfect time to introduce this unit because children will be able to use everything they learned during the previous two units of study to write fiction well. This unit can provide you with opportunities to increase expectations for writing volume and stamina in your class-room. You can support children to write longer stories in part by shrinking the size of the planning pictures children make, or by encouraging some children to jot a quick phrase in each of those planning boxes instead of relying on drawing, which is a more time-consuming vehicle for planning. You may want to provide paper with more lines per page.

As you head into the unit, be clear that children will write lots of stories during this month, each working at his or her own pace. Some may write three stories, while others will write four, five, or more! Remember that if you teach students how to generate ideas for stories and ways to write the leads, they will be able to draw on this repertoire of strategies (plus all the strategies they learned during previous years) whenever the time comes for them to start a new story, to write a first page, and so forth.

Help Students Generate Story Ideas

Early in the unit, if your students wrote fiction the year before, ask them to recall what they already know about writing fiction. You could ask children to bring in stories they wrote last year, if they have those saved at home, or you can have them tell partners about those stories. You'll need to decide what you want children to do that they did the year before and what you want them to do that is new. The TCRWP staff tends to suggest you continue to channel kids to write about characters who are roughly their ages. You can decide whether you want to invite children to portray those main characters as animals if they choose to do so. Lots of children's books use raccoons or foxes or rabbits to portray children, and some of your second graders might want to do the same.

This year you might teach your children that before they devote a day or two to character development, drawing and writing notes about the character, it can help to brainstorm story lines. A child might write, for example, "I could write about a kid who moves and has no friends and then gets a friend somehow. I could write about a kid who wants to make a goal in soccer and then does."

Many teachers have their second graders bring out the Tiny Topics Notepads they used during the previous unit of study and carry these once again, this time thinking of and jotting story ideas. As a child waits for the school bus, he might write down, "Misses bus and walks to school." As the child heads off to art class, he can write, "Boy makes great painting in art and wins prize."

Support Your Students as They Develop Their Characters and Stories

Once a student has decided upon a story idea—"Kid makes a soccer goal and team wins the trophy"—she will be more apt to angle the character development in such a way that it fits with the story idea. The main character in the soccer story may be a terrific athlete, or may not be, and this decision, and ones like it, are all bound in with the story line.

After teaching children to generate ideas for a story and to choose one, teach them to think through how the story might go. Encourage children to tell the story across their fingers or to say it aloud as they turn the pages of a blank booklet, and to do this multiple times across one day's writing workshop. Too many second graders get the idea for a story and, because they are less worried about the actual writing part of authorship, plunge immediately into writing page 1. Page 1, however, binds the writer into a story line (especially because these youngsters are not yet keen on the idea of writing multiple drafts). The only solution, then, is to emphasize the importance of telling a story multiple times—and of telling the story multiple ways, too—before writing it.

You may want to suggest children use planning booklets. These need to be very informal—no dittoed storyboards, please! You can simply show children how to take a sheet of paper and fold it in half, then fold that half into half. There will now be four pages in this booklet. Suggest that each child take half a minute to sketch how the story might go, with each page representing one part of the story. The story about the boy winning a soccer goal could start on page 1 with a stick-figure boy kicking the ball into the goal; no words are necessary. The writer would then need to figure out what should occupy the next three pages. Is the boy treated like a hero by his teammates—and if so, how, exactly? Then what happens on page 3? The point of these planning booklets is that it takes all of three minutes to sketch a storybook, from start to finish, so this means a child can sketch a couple of versions for how the story might go, storytelling each (touching the page and saying aloud the exact words the writer might write). Don't imagine this as more than the work of one writing workshop, but do imagine that during rehearsal for writing, at least some of your writers will actually revise before writing a single word. The important thing is that writers benefit from trying a story one way and then another way, deciding how the story should go out of an awareness of options. Once the writer has a plan for the story, she can shift to a regular booklet, with a place on each page for a sketch or a phrase or two and with lots of lines for writing.

As children do this work, teach them that generally the character wants something and then gets into trouble on her way to achieving the goal. That is, if the story is about a girl who wants to visit her grandmother in South America, the writer should ask, "What might get in the way of that trip?" Does her father have a strained relationship with his mother (the girl's grandmother) and not want her to go? Does the girl have a fear of flying in an airplane? Is her family unable to buy her a plane ticket?

The other big challenge is that children will want to summarize rather than storytell the story. The writer will decide, "This is a story about a girl who wants a cell phone and doesn't have the money and then she gets it." Once the writer comes up with the story line, he begins writing: "Amy wanted a cell phone. 'Can I have one?' she asked. Her mother said no because they didn't have the money. Then one day she was walking to school and she saw something and it was a cell phone." End of story.

In order to teach children to storytell rather than summarize, it is crucial for you to teach them that they need to think, "What, exactly, will be happening at the start of my story? If the girl wants a cell phone, what exactly is she doing to show this? If this were a play, what would she be doing on stage?" Perhaps the child decides that the main character is writing her Christmas list.

Next the writer needs to make a movie in his mind of the exact story and begin reimagining it. "Emily bent low over the paper and whispered, 'Cell, cell, cell,' as she wrote. On the page, she wrote c-e-l. Then she said, 'Phone, phone,' and soon she'd written, in her best spelling, 'Cel-fone.' Emily got up and went to the refrigerator and stuck her Christmas list under a magnet. 'Mom,' she said, 'my Christmas list only has one thing on it.' "

All the advice you might give children to include characters' feelings or to make characters talk is almost inconsequential compared with the absolutely crucial importance of teaching kids to relive the story as they write, imagining the story unfold bit by bit.

One of the best ways to help children imagine a story is to encourage the writer to act out the story, then record what she does. You may want to use partnership time as a time for children to reenact key scenes in the stories they are writing. In this way, a writer chooses a scene to reenact, bit by bit, to bring her story to life and give words to action and dialogue. Meanwhile, her partner can help put words to paper as the movement grows into story. The partnership can revisit this same scene to elaborate or they can share different scenes to get to know characters and their motivations. This partnership can be an ongoing structure throughout the unit, through drafting and revision.

It is important to remind children that they need to use all that they know about narrative writing in order to write their stories as well as possible. For example, if during the Small Moment unit of study, you taught children that narrative writers sometimes begin a story by conveying the weather, or by showing the main character doing or saying something very specific, then during this unit of study, you'll remind children of what they learned about ways to begin a story. The only difference is that instead of writing, "I took off my sneakers and ran barefoot across the beach to the edge of the water," they will now write, "Waldo took off his sneakers and ran barefoot to the edge of the water." Likewise, you'll remind children that when they revise fiction, they can draw on the exact same techniques they used for revision of personal narratives.

It is important to remind children to draw on all they learned about craft from mentor authors so their stories merit being read aloud. As you teach, keep in mind, too, the results of your narrative assessment. What are your children able to do on their own? What can they almost but not quite do? Teach toward skills just beyond your children's reach.

Expand Students' Repertoire of Strategies and Intentions for Revision

After children devote three weeks to rehearsing, drafting, and revising a couple of stories, ask them to choose their best—and then surprise them with the news that once writers have selected our best, we make the best even better. We reread our first thoughts and see gaps in them. We look again and see connections between two different sets of ideas. Through rereading and revision, writing becomes a tool for thinking. A commitment to revision is part and parcel of a commitment to writing as a process. Revision is a complement to good writing.

You can easily rally children to revise by giving them special revision tools and materials: a revision folder and a colored pen, swatches of paper on which they can add paragraphs into their drafts, and flaps of paper that can be taped over parts of the story they decide to revise. Teach them to use staple removers, if they don't already use these regularly, so they can make their books longer or shorter.

Of course the physical tools of revision are useless without the knowledge of *how* to revise. One of the most important ways to steer second graders to revise is by elaborating. If a child wrote, "For my birthday, I got a bike," teach this child that he can cross out that summary of the event and instead storytell what happened, step-by-step. In order to go from a summary line to a detailed narrative, the writer needs to do more than add on information. Injunctions to do so lead to pages like this: "For my birthday, I got a bike. It was red and has a basket. I liked it. I was happy. It was a great, great bike." Instead, show children how to use dialogue to create a feeling of story and how to build suspense: "On my birthday, Dad said, 'Cover your eyes.' Then I heard him opening some doors, moving some things. 'Open your eyes!' he called. I opened them and saw my dad wheeling a red bike into the room. . . ."

It may be too much to ask a child to revise each and every page so extensively, so you may want to teach children to reread their pieces, asking themselves, "Which page is the most important?" If kids have a hard time figuring out the most important part of a story, they might instead ask themselves, "Where in my story does the main character have the biggest feelings?" Once the child has identified that part, she can rewrite that page from top to bottom, this time reliving the moment and depicting it with details.

You can also teach students to create more literary beginnings or endings to their stories. Children can try writing a few different versions of a lead or an ending (or any part of their story) and then think about which version works best. Children may want to study mentor texts the class has read, trying to name what the writer did in his or her beginning or ending. For example, children might reread the ending of *Fireflies!* and recognize that Julie Brinckloe ends the piece with a strong feeling.

> I held the jar, dark and empty,
> in my hands.
> The moonlight and the fireflies
> swam in my tears,
>
> but I could feel myself smiling.

In fact, the feeling is conflicted, the moment bittersweet; the narrator is crying, mourning the loss of her fireflies, but she is smiling, too, knowing the fireflies are alive now that she's set them free. Children could then end their own piece in a similar way. They could try to end their piece by demonstrating conflicting feelings—or one powerful feeling—in several ways.

Similarly, children might notice that another author starts off her writing by describing the setting, using weather to elicit the feeling of the piece. Children could then try setting up their story in similar ways, thinking about how their characters are feeling in the story and describing the weather so that it matches that emotion.

A Cause for Celebration

One of the nicest ways to celebrate students' fiction writing is to add these books to the classroom library with the same reverence given to other new books. Children could imagine categories and design labels for baskets that will hold their precious stories. For example, if several students wrote a story with an animal as the main character, there could be an "Animal Characters" basket. Maybe a few students wrote stories about sports, so they might name and label a basket "Stories About the Big Game." These baskets could take up space in a new section of the classroom library, and you might decide to have a little book release party, with snacks and mingling.

The World of Wonder

Fairy Tale Adaptations and Original Fantasy Stories

This unit invites children to write either several adaptations of one fairy tale or an adaptation of several different fairy tales. Although the children will believe the unit is all about fairy tales and you will certainly help them learn about how these stories tend to go, your real purpose for the unit is to deepen your children's abilities to write in general and more specifically to write stories that incorporate literary language and elements of narrative craft. Before teaching this unit, you may want to reread the description of November's unit on fiction writing because this unit will allow you to cycle your children back through much of that work, this time helping them write more skillfully and work more independently. That is, just as October invited children to revisit September's work with personal narrative writing, this unit will invite children to revisit November's work with fiction writing.

In this unit as in the previous one, children will take a day or perhaps even two days to plan a story before writing it. One of the most important ways to rehearse for writing a story is to reconsider where, in the sequence of events, the story will begin and what, exactly, the main character will be doing or saying when the story starts. After settling on a starting point for the story and a likely sequence of events, the child will sketch a tiny picture onto each page of a story booklet (by this time each page of those booklets will contain lots and lots of lines and just a very small space for a planning sketch) and then will touch each page and storytell the whole story of that particular page.

Then the writer will write, writing on lots and lots of lines per page, and as the writer writes, he will envision the story, making a movie in his mind, almost becoming the main character, mentally acting out what the character does, thinks, and says, while scribing this mental movie onto the page. Of course, once a writer has written one story, he will either engage in significant revisions—this time, even perhaps a whole new draft—or move on to write another story.

Children will begin to do all that familiar work of writing stories *after* you have introduced them to a few fairy tales, one of which they will adapt.

Coming to Know a Fairy Tale or Two Very Well

This unit aims to give children a grasp for the reoccurring, persisting elements in fairy tales. And it aims to give your students a way to know a few fairy tales deeply, so those tales become part of who they are. Prior to the unit, we suggest you read and reread several versions of one, two, or three fairy tales. Then, at the start of this unit, during read-aloud time, reread variations of the one tale that you select as your first focus. Select variations that hug the shores of the original text, not ones that are told from different points of view (as in the Wolf's version of *The Three Little Pigs*—save that for later).

Your second graders may have heard a fairy tale or two—maybe even many—but chances are they haven't yet internalized the common elements of fairy tales. They probably have yet to sense that in fairy tales, for example, things tend to come in threes—three wishes, three pigs, and incantations uttered three times. They probably haven't yet absorbed the fact that usually fairy tales begin "Once upon a time, long, long ago" and then show that in some setting, in some situation, there lived someone with an unusual trait. They may not yet know the predictable rhythms of these stories, such as the fact that the main character will probably have cares, worries, or wants, and these will probably lead to troubles. They probably have yet to learn that in fairy tales, the good tends to win over bad, and that as often as not, the younger, the smaller, the unlikely person rises to the occasion and saves the day, usually outwitting the far stronger opponent. Then, too, most of your second graders will only this year make the spectacular discovery that the same tale can be told in many ways. As you read fairy tales to your children, you'll want to engage children in talking about how these tales tend to go. You can let them in on some of the underlying features of fairy tales so they feel as if they've been given insider information, but of course they'll especially love coming to their own discoveries about fairy tales.

Rehearsing and Drafting Adaptations of Fairy Tales

As you gather children to listen to adaptations of the tale you've selected, let them know that in a day or two, every child will have a chance to write his own adaptation of that tale. Suggest they listen, thinking about how they could adapt the tale, and take time to turn and talk with a partner, swapping ideas for how the same story could be told a bit differently. Perhaps some of them will change the setting from countryside to city, others will alter the characters from boys to girls or from pigs to cats. When your children share ideas they're beginning to develop for how they will adapt the story, show them that any one change a child makes will lead to others. If a child is writing a variation on *The Three Billy Goats Gruff*, and has turned the goats into raccoons, they will not be trip-trapping across a bridge to get to a meadow! Will they skitter across the bridge? If their destination is changed to a garbage can in the alley, will they cross a porch instead of a bridge?

Next, help children begin rehearsing to write their own renditions of the fairy tale. Encourage them to return to all they know about rehearsing for fiction writing, but to also return to the existing tale repeatedly to scaffold their authorship of the new version. Give each partnership a copy of the text (of one version of it, anyhow) and encourage partners to reread and rethink the text. Don't worry if many of your children cannot actually read the words. As long as you have read the tale at least three times, they can use the pictures and their memories of the text to re-create the general sequence, which is all they will need in order to imagine how the text could go differently.

As children imagine how they might tell the tale differently, you may want to give them some quick lessons on reading critically. Authors rewrite traditional tales for reasons. Sometimes we rewrite a familiar tale because we disagree with the way the tale stereotyped or that the real prize worth going after is money or food—we may want the prize to be world peace or ways to help others. Sometimes authors rewrite a tale to make it more relevant to readers who live in cities or to be more appealing to children. Help children mull over their options. During the workshop, partnerships can reread a version of a fairy tale and talk about the choices the author made and the choices they could imagine reconsidering.

Of course, most of this work will center less on mulling over decisions and more on imagining the implications of any one of those decisions. If one child wants to remake *The Three Little Pigs* as *The Three Little Dogs*, that child will probably question whether the villain should still be a hungry wolf. Might it be an eager dog catcher? Similarly, would the story still be set in the country, or might it be in a city?

Children will probably need more than the four pages they used during the last unit for planning, so you may suggest they begin with not one but two sheets of paper, folding these over as described in the fiction unit.

The work described so far will probably require two or three days at the start of this unit, and none of those days will involve a lot of actual writing. As children rehearse, use conferences and small-group work to channel them toward the actual writing. You may find that some of your especially proficient second graders should in fact be writing on lined notebook paper—fold a page over at its waistline, and this in itself creates booklets containing four half pages. Be sure children sketch or jot a word in a corner of each page, signifying that on that page the child will tell the whole story—the beginning, middle, and end—of just the one event that is represented by that icon. The author may need additional pages, which is fine. Be sure when the child goes to write, that each page is written a bit like a Small Moment story, with the writer starting by thinking, "What exactly is this character doing at the start of this episode?"

While teaching any unit of study, you and your colleagues will gather to consider the predictable problems that children are apt to encounter. Anticipate that the challenge of helping children storytell rather than summarize will be an enduring one and have a repertoire of teaching strategies that you draw upon to help children draft and revise toward this goal (also called showing, not telling). Remember you can suggest children reenact (dramatize) and then write, you can suggest children storytell repeatedly, and so on. If you are expecting children to revise a summarized story so as to make it a storytold one, know that this will probably require an entirely new draft. If a child tries to simply add a few details onto a summary, the resulting text will likely not be much better than the first one.

Revising the Fairy Tale—or Writing Another

Each of your second graders will write a handful of stories during this month. You will need to decide whether these will continue to be variations of the original fairy tale you selected or whether children will tackle another fairy tale altogether. If they do the latter, you need to decide whether this will be another fairy tale that you've read aloud and discussed with lots of whole-class work or whether the children's work with the next fairy tale will be more independent. As is always the case with curricular decisions, each choice will have its own possibilities and its own limitations.

If you decide to invest another week or two in having children work with the one fairy tale they've already adapted, encourage them to reread the adaptation they've already written, and remind them that writers write not just one draft, but several drafts, before a story is done. Suggest that this time, children reread the original story noticing not only the broad choices the author made but the details of craft—that is, noticing not only that the characters in *The Three Billy Goats Gruff* are goats but also the techniques the author used to write the original text.

Your writers can bring out the template of craft charts they used when apprenticing themselves earlier this year to mentor authors, and once again, they can read their new mentor text noticing places where the fairy tale made an impact on them, making them feel something or see something. Then they can ask that question they have learned to ask, "What exactly did the author do to create this effect?"

Children will notice qualities of good writing that you hope writers emulate often, as well as peculiarities of the text under study. Help youngsters think, "Why might the author have decided to write this way?" and "What would the text be like if the author had written it differently?" and "Are there places in my own writing where I could try my hand at something similar?"

There are many things that you will probably hope your children will study and emulate. For example, fairy tale writers often incorporate a certain kind of literary language, using phrases such as "Once upon a time" and "But then, one day" or "Not long after that." Fairy tale writers often write with complex sentences. Instead of writing, "He did this and then he did that and then he did this and then he did that," fairy tale writers often begin a sentence by telling when or where or under what conditions or with what sorts of feelings someone did something. For example: "Just after the little goat reached the other side of the bridge, the middle goat took a step toward the bridge." Another example: "Worrying that the troll would appear again, the middle goat walked quickly across the bridge."

Fairy tales are almost invariably structured like classic stories, with a character wanting something, running into trouble, and finally figuring out a way to tackle the trouble. Children can turn to the story the class has studied together to see if this structure undergirds that story. Then they can ask, "Does that same structure brace my rendition of the tale?" Fairy tales also usually contain a fairly heavy-handed moral; thus they provide children with chances to practice highlighting a meaning or moral.

There will be other aspects of published fairy tales that you wish to highlight. Your decision will come from reading over student drafts and thinking, "What gets in the way of these being better?" and "What do many students seem to be on the brink of being able to do?" Remember that qualities of good writing need to be turned into processes. So, for example, if the characters in many of your children's stories seem similar to each other, you might suggest to writers that they act out a scene from their stories during a partnership share, thinking carefully about how each character walks or talks. The goats trip-trap across the bridge, but how does the troll move? Surely he doesn't trip-trap! Once children have acted out the ways that one character moves differently than another, then they can reach for the precisely accurate words to depict what they envision.

Instead of suggesting children write, revise, and even write second drafts of their fairy tale rendition, you could suggest they try writing an entirely different version of that familiar story. Alternately, you could suggest that after all your children write their own variation of a fairy tale that you read to them, they continue to do the same work with another fairy tale that they choose on their own and pursue with more independence.

If you opt to encourage second graders to tackle a second and perhaps even a third fairy tale, writing a new version of each, be sure to leave time for some of the revision work described earlier. Perhaps before the last week of the unit, invite children to reread all the fairy tales they have written, selecting their best for further revisions.

One final point: This unit will mark the end of four months of work with narrative writing, so you will want to end the unit with another day of assessment. Go back to the start of this book and reread the directions for assessing narrative writing. Give children the same amount of time, and once again keep your hands off, refraining from hints and reminders. In addition to assessing student writing, you should celebrate it; invent your own wonderful ideas for doing so.

Writing to Grow Ideas
(Including Ideas About Books)

My sister recently adopted an eight-year-old from an orphanage in Russia. When I asked her what Karil had said about the differences between Russia and America, my sister responded, "He doesn't have the English to talk about those things."

So I asked, "Well, when he goes to the Russian translator, what does he say?"

My sister thought for a moment and then said, "I don't think he has the *Russian* to talk about those sorts of ideas either. When he was in the orphanage in Russia, I don't think many people asked him for his opinion on things." Many of our children, including our English-speaking children, are equally unaccustomed to putting ideas into words.

As adults, we know the deep pleasure that comes from sharing an idea with one person, another, another, and feeling that idea grow from wisps of thought into something that feels close to the core of who we are. We know the thrill that comes from changing our mind—from teasing out the inconsistencies in what we are saying, following the ramifications, and seeing the contradictions within our thinking. We know that others can help us take apart the threads of our thinking and can inspire us, too, to follow a line of thought. Children, however, are still learning to find words that capture thoughts, hopes, ideas. They are learning to frame opinions, to question their first ideas, to refine their positions.

This unit aims to help children find pleasure in the process of reaching for the words that capture their ideas, insights, questions, wonderings. The unit aims to show second graders that it is a great joy to think about experiences, about the stuff of our lives, about subjects in the world, and, yes, about the contents of books, too. In this way, the unit teaches children to comprehend—that is, to infer, predict, entertain questions, interpret—and to do all this as they watch clouds race across the sky, as they think back upon the moments of their lives, and as they reflect upon Poppleton's relationship with Cherry Sue.

This unit is a new one for teachers in the Teachers College Reading and Writing Project thought collaborative, and we hope that teachers across the world join us in exploring the potential in the ideas that I sketch out over the next few pages.

Getting Started

We imagine the unit will begin with you telling kids that they've become really good at writing stories and then saying, "But writers do not write only stories. We also write ideas, and during this unit of study, we'll explore ways that writers can write about ideas. We can have ideas about our own lives, and ideas about the lives of characters in the books that we read, and ideas about stuff in the world like wasps' nests and car engines—and this month, we'll try our hand at growing and writing ideas about all sorts of stuff."

Before issuing such an invitation, you need to clarify in your own mind what it is that you imagine children will actually produce in this unit. That is, what will the texts themselves look like? What genre are you expecting youngsters to produce? What mentor texts do you have that resemble the sort of thing you hope kids will write?

The truth is, I'm not totally sure what the work that kids produce in this unit will be like. I could, of course, feign certainty for the purpose of winning over your confidence, but I think it is important to acknowledge that teaching is a form of inquiry, and that it is not unusual for teachers and kids to embark on a unit of study expecting the unexpected. Having said that, of course I have possibilities in mind. I'm imagining that at least at first, you'll invite youngsters to keep miniature, short-term writer's notebooks. They'll write entries, just as I've written about at length in *Living Between the Lines* (1990). The mystery, for me, is that I'm not sure whether it will seem important to help youngsters go from collecting lots of entries to selecting one of them and developing it into a publishable text. I am not sure whether every child will find her own form, one that suits the child's topic and vision, or whether you will steer children toward a specific form, and if so, what that form will be.

During the first week of the unit, children will reread the Small Moment stories they wrote earlier and then write *patches of thoughts* off those narratives. One child might reread an account she wrote in October about the time she watched her apartment packed into a moving truck, and now, months later, she might write an entry about her thoughts and feelings about moving. When we first ask children to write thoughts and feelings, it is typical for them to write only briefly. Although it is easy for a child who is writing the sequence of events she experienced to write on and on and on, it is less easy to write on and on when writing about one's ideas. The child is apt to write a line or two—say, "It was sad"—and then put the pen down.

Support Children in Thinking More and Saying More About Their Ideas

You will need to help children say more, and, more importantly, think more and revise by adding on. You'll probably need to teach them that often writers write a line or two about how we felt and then try another way to capture that feeling, aiming for more precision. Sometimes this simply means that we write, "I miss that old house," and then add the words *That is*, and try to say the same thing differently. "I miss that old house. *That is*, I am lonely for that old house." This can continue. "*In other words*, it is like part of me is still back in the house that used to be mine."

In order to help children find more precise ways to capture a feeling or an idea, you might help them use more nuanced vocabulary by teaching them lists of words—word scales, really—that describe feelings along a spectrum of intensity, from mild to extreme. For example, the child who is yearning for her old home might consider a list ranging from unhappy to heartbroken. When the child discovers her parents plan to move, she may feel glum. When she has to say good-bye to her best friend on moving day, she may feel downright heartbroken. Then, too, you can help children learn that often there are no single words to capture a feeling or an idea, and this is why writers reach for metaphor. "I felt like a porcupine— prickly outside and soft inside."

You might well be thinking, "This is beyond my kids," and that is probably true—putting ideas into words is hard for all of us—but we invite second graders to do lots of other challenging work such as authoring books and emulating world-class authors, and that work is also well beyond them. Children benefit from the invitation to try as best they can to write their own dawning insights and to capture their ideas.

You can teach children that as we write about our thoughts and feelings, we often find new ideas come into our mind, and soon writing itself is generating ideas. Many second graders think of the process of writing as one that involves getting an idea into mind and then freezing it for as long as it takes to record that idea. In this unit, this means that you will repeatedly teach children that they can get started writing without having a plan for where the words will lead. So the child writing about moving day might write, "I'm surprised that I . . . ," and not know what it was that did surprise her about that moving day. By the time she is ready to write the second half of that sentence, words will have surfaced, thoughts will have come.

Children will also need you to teach them that writers alternate between writing generalizations and writing specifics, between advocating ideas and supplying evidence. If children at the start of this unit reread Small Moment narratives they wrote earlier in the year and write big ideas that circle those moments, they will already have both big ideas and an illustrative example.

Help Writers Grow Ideas About the World Around Them

This part of the unit might involve children doing similar work but, this time, writing their ideas about objects from the natural world. Perhaps, as part of your science curriculum, your children will already have been studying plants or the street corner on which your school building stands. Whatever it is you have been studying, chances are good there are aspects of that topic that are physical and are present in your room or can be seen from your classroom. Teach children that just as writers reread our writing and think, "What ideas does this story spark in me?" similarly, writers study stuff that interests us—the people coming in and out of a bakery, the buds on a tree—and we think, "What ideas does this spark in me?"

Children will again need help elaborating on their ideas. Remind them of what you have already taught during the beginning of the unit. Your teaching needs to be cumulative, and you should see that the entries that your children write now are much more elaborated upon from the start than those they wrote even just a week ago at the start of the unit. Then, too, the revision work that you prompted earlier should now be something your kids can do with less prompting from you. You'll also want to use this time as an opportunity to extend what your kids can do as they write about feelings and ideas. Perhaps now you want to emphasize writing to think, showing kids that one idea can lead to another. All of us know the game in which one person says a word (e.g., *dog*) and then next person says whatever comes to mind (*obedience*), then the first says the new word that comes to mind (*rules*) and the next person follows (*my mother*). Learning to let writing lead us to new ideas involves a process that is not entirely different from that game of free association. We write a sentence or two, then think of whatever we've said for an instant, knowing as we do this that something related, some further thought, will fill our mind. We write that new thought . . . and one thing leads to the next.

Sometimes it helps to teach children a few phrases that help us explore ideas: "The surprising thing about this is . . . ," "This makes me realize . . . ," "The new idea I'm getting is . . . ," "I'm starting to think that . . . ," "This is important because . . . ," "This reminds me of . . ." Notice that none of these phrases channels writers toward supplying specific examples; these instead are thought prompts that keep writers at the level of ideas. It is also, however, worthwhile to teach youngsters to shift between generalizations and specifics, as mentioned earlier, and there are other thought prompts that can accomplish that job ("For example," "For instance").

Partnerships will need to fuel a lot of the thinking in this unit. Every unit of study will pose its own challenges, and in this unit, children could say, "I don't have anything to say," and "I don't have any ideas about . . ." All of us know that the best way to grow ideas is to participate in a provocative conversation on the topic, and you will want to use partnerships as a forum to support children rehearsing for writing by having grand conversations about whatever their subjects are. Partnership conversations can help a child revise his writing to incorporate the new thinking. You may also teach partners to push each other's thinking by developing each idea that is discussed. If your partnership conversations usually consist of one child saying one idea and then the other child saying another unrelated idea, teach children to discuss one idea for a bit before continuing on to another. Encourage children to press each other to say more, to think more, saying things like, "Why is that important?" "Why do you think that?" and "Is there another possibility?"

Sometimes it can help to teach children that they can think like a scientist or think like a historian (depending on the topic they are studying). For example, if children are looking closely at plants and writing their ideas about plants, you can teach them that it helps to think like scientists. "What patterns do I see—what similarities and differences do I notice—among these trees?" Similar questions could be asked about the neighborhood.

The writing that children do during this segment of the unit could be collected in their writer's notebooks alongside writing about the children's experiences, although it is also conceivable that children could write nonfiction books with titles such as "My Ideas About Crickets" or "Observations, Wonderings, and Ideas About Crickets" or "My Tree Book."

Support Writers to Grow Ideas About Their Reading

In the final part of this unit, you will want to help children do similar work in order to grow ideas sparked by the books they're reading. There will be tremendous power simply to the notion that children can bring the habits of mind they've used earlier to now help them think about books. Then, too, you can say to your kids, "Earlier you looked at plants through the eyes of scientists. Now I want to teach you how to look at books through the eyes of good readers." This can then serve as a prelude for you to teach kids any of the ways in which good readers look at books—you choose what specific lenses you want to give your children! For example, you might teach them that readers notice patterns in books and think about why those patterns exist. You might teach them that readers notice how characters change from the beginning to the end of a book and think, "How do the changes that this character made relate to what the book is really mostly about?" The important thing for you to keep in mind is that your goal for now is not to turn your seven-year-olds into kids who are ready to take the SAT exam. You are not hoping your children will write tidy little five-paragraph essays about books. Instead, you are hoping that kids become comfortable growing ideas about texts and capturing those ideas on the page.

A Plan for the Rest of the Year

B y February, the year will be well launched. For the remaining pages of this book, let's cast a long glance forward, imagining a progression of further units that might allow your children to continue developing their abilities and aspirations as writers.

Certainly for at least one upcoming unit and I'd suggest for two units, children need the opportunity to write informational texts. I'd imagine a February unit of study designed to help children write informational books on topics of personal choice and interest, and then a later unit—perhaps in May—in which children revisit that work, this time writing informational books within a whole-class science or social studies inquiry.

In addition, it is always important to design units of study that invite children to decide what writing they want to do and to progress with a great deal of independence, working toward goals they set. This could be called a unit on independent writing projects, or alternatively, the unit could invite independence but shine a spotlight on an aspect of the writing process. The TCRWP community decided to take up that goal, with a unit on revision, one that aimed to also support increasing independence.

For me and for many teachers, it goes without question that children need opportunities to write poetry. The poetry unit described in *Units of Study for Primary Writing* (Calkins et al. 2003) has wingspan enough to support your second graders (even your third graders) in a poetry unit. You'll want to reimagine other units, however, so that they provide rising expectations so they can continue to take your youngsters as far as they can go.

So that leaves just one remaining month, and my colleagues and I have recently devoted that month to a unit of study on persuasive writing, one that invites children to write persuasive letters and reviews of restaurants, TV shows, movies, toys, and books.

This, then, cumulates into a spring curriculum that looks like this:

February	Expert Projects: Writing to Learn and to Teach About a Topic of Personal Expertise
March	Persuasive Writing: Persuasive Letters and Reviews
April	Poetry
May	Expert Projects in a Content Area: Writing to Learn and to Teach About Science
June	Revision and Assessment

The course of study I've just outlined could progress differently. For example, this particular yearlong journey does not include as much work in narrative writing as I generally think is wise, and therefore I could easily argue for a return to personal narrative writing, perhaps in a unit called Edge-of-the-Seat Stories, which would be designed to help children write stories that contain a lot of tension. As I mentioned earlier, I could easily have devoted a month to independent writing projects or, if I wanted to highlight reading-writing connections during that month, to author studies (or mentor text studies). Lately it seems that many of the nation's best-selling books are How-To books: how to train your dog, how to lead an organization, how to lose weight. I could imagine ratcheting up the expectations in the primary How-To book work, inviting children to write a richly developed How-To book. All of these units assume that children are working in partnerships, but none of the units actually shines a spotlight on partnerships, and I could well imagine a unit that does so. The point is: Go at it! Convene a group of colleagues and tackle the exhilarating project of designing a unit of study for yourselves—and then share it with the rest of us!

Expert Projects

If you decide to follow the curricular calendar my colleagues and I have adopted, then you'll want to begin by thinking about ways in which a unit on expert projects can extend the work your children did previously when working on

All-About books. In the kindergarten and first-grade classrooms we know best, during the All-About unit, children tend to crank out loads of little All-About books. In the unit on Expert Projects, children instead spend a portion of the unit writing to learn about their subject and then a portion writing to teach. That is, children select a topic and then persist with it for a whole month (for seven-year-olds, this is a long time!). Make a big deal of this because it is important for children to feel that this month marks an essential rite of passage. Fire them up with a drumroll about the fact that now that they're almost third graders, they need to realize that people have an obligation to teach others what they know. Climax the unit with a gigantic Expert Project fair, and during that fair, other children—first graders, other second graders—can come to tiny seminars taught by second graders, convening with a few listeners in all corners of the gym, the school foyer, or the school library.

You could teach particular strategies that writers use to generate ideas for expertise reports, but the strategies are trivial next to the importance of creating classrooms in which writers feel heard. It will be important for you to help children feel a sense of authority about topics they think ordinary. If one child's mother just had a baby, that child may need you to help him realize that the rest of us would love to know what it's been like to have a baby in the family. If another child recently moved from Haiti to the United States, help that youngster understand that his expertise is precious indeed. Be prepared to be a student of your students, listening with responsiveness to any topic they throw out. There is nothing like a rapt listener to help any one of us realize that we *do* in fact have lessons to teach.

You may want to subtly guide your stronger writers to more focused (and more challenging) topics. It will be easier to devote a month to soccer than to the role of the goalie, but the latter topic will probably yield better writing.

Teach your students that when we are experts on a topic, we do not simply turn around and teach others. Instead we become avid learners. To help children become learners, you may want to suggest they bring artifacts related to their topic to school, creating a shoebox collection. One child can bring baseball cards, another photographs of a dog. Children can sketch things they can't bring to school. Then children can use the writing skills they developed during the previous month, writing lots of entries in a little subject-specific miniature writer's notebook. The goal can be for each child to write smart, original, important, fresh ideas about whatever subject she wants to teach others about. As part of this, writers will need to ask and probe questions, and to become researchers, finding books and authorities to learn from.

Your unit will take a turn after a bit, and you'll challenge children to take all they know and think and begin imagining writing a collection of texts designed to teach others about this topic. Read aloud some informational writing and use your own expertise project as a model. You'll probably want to spotlight texts that have tables of contents and that contain different chapters, each of which takes up a different aspect of the subject, as categorizing information is crucial in informational writing. You may want to sort the published informational writing into different piles so that children learn an array of possible organizational structures. Show them that some texts follow a question-answer structure. Others are written as narratives, with lots of information embedded into a story related to the topic ("How I Chose My New Puppy"). The wonderful thing is that once you design a unit on expertise projects, you can reuse that unit plan a second time, this time asking children to all select a subtopic related to a whole-class science or social studies theme.

Persuasive Writing

There are lots of reasons why a persuasive writing unit is perfect for seven- and eight-year-olds. First of all, these youngsters deserve to know that words matter, that writing can make a difference in the world. They're apt to care about writing if writing accomplishes real jobs in the world. Consider how powerful it is for a child to write the mayor, suggesting that speed bumps need to be added to a certain road—and for those speed bumps to be actually installed. Imagine the sense of confidence a child might develop if he took up a cause—promoting recycling across the school, suggesting children should be able to walk from the playground to the classroom without staying within a regimented line, adding more books to a class library—and the child's own advocacy led to changes in the world. What an important lesson for citizens who all too often feel silenced and powerless rather than encouraged to raise their voices to make the world a better place.

But this unit is important also because it gives children opportunities to develop the muscles they're going to need soon when they are called upon to write literary essays and to answer document-based questions—and they'll need these muscles not only within their writing workshop but also across the curriculum and in high-stakes testing situations.

My colleague Sarah Picard Taylor wrote *A Quick Guide to Teaching Persuasive Writing, K–2* (2008), a book in this series that details how a unit on persuasive writing might progress. If you don't yet have that book, here is one way a unit on persuasive writing may go. You might begin by having children consider issues that matter to them in their classroom, their school, their families and then write letters in which they make a claim about the issue and provide support for it. "Dear Mr. Principal," a child can write. "Our classroom needs more good series books!" In such a letter, the young advocate will find that she is most persuasive if she tells small stories to make her case, embedding anecdotes into the letter. She'll learn that it is powerful to anticipate objections and to address them: "You might be thinking . . . ," she can write, and head off any counterarguments. Then, too, persuasive letter writers may find it helps to spell out the practical details for the proposed plan.

The writing muscles that are called for when writing persuasive letters are similar to those called for in a review. In reviews as in letters, the writer makes and supports a claim, using and angling evidence to be convincing. The writer addresses a reader and needs to keep the reader's questions and counterarguments in mind.

Writing Projects: Self-Assessment, Revision, and Writing with Independence

Imagine starting this unit by bringing out the writing that children did at the very start of the year and suggesting they look back on it and think about whether they could revise some of that early writing, making it *so* much better! Just think of the zeal with which children will go at the task of improving what they'll clearly look upon with distain as "baby writing." How they will flex their writing muscles, when encouraged to show how much more they know about writing well, how much more they can do.

The children's revisions won't begin to fit into flaps and inserted words. They'll clearly need to write whole new drafts of those old stories. Peek ahead to the *Units of Study for Teaching Writing, Grades 3–5* books (Calkins et al. 2006) and specifically to "Launching the Writing Workshop" so that you can tuck in some topics about how third graders go about planning for a story, getting ready to write, drafting, and revising. But mostly, encourage children to write their new drafts on books in which each page is either a whole or a half sheet of regular notebook paper (perhaps the pages holding the heart of the story, presumably the middle pages, will be whole pages and the early and late ones will be half pages). Encourage children to storytell their narratives to each other multiple times before writing, making sure each story starts with a precise action or dialogue ("I opened the car door, got out, and stood on the hot sand. 'Race you to the ocean,' I said."). Encourage children to retell their stories many times, trying to make listeners really feel what they want them to feel, helping listeners really picture the whole thing. Let them write their drafts "long and strong," writing lickety-split down the page.

Once children have rewritten their early stories as more developed narratives, you may want to lean on "The Craft of Revision" book in *Units of Study for Primary Writing* (Calkins et al. 2003). You can encourage children to revise those whole new drafts, and you can also remind them that sometimes, as part of revision, writers take a draft and imagine writing about the same content using a whole new genre. A story could become a poem, a song, a persuasive letter, a nonfiction book. Your children will graduate from second grade soon and head off to their summers, and your best hope is that they leave you all fired up about writing. You'll want to end the year by especially fostering a sense of independence. If a child loves Calvin and Hobbes cartoons, maybe that child wants to actually devote a chunk of his summer to writing a takeoff on those books. Perhaps another child is gearing up to write her very own chapter book. Maybe yet another wants to write an anthology of poems.

You'll ask, "What's the teaching I can do when children are embarking on their own individual writing projects?" and the answer is that you can teach children the life of being a writer and the process of planning for and carrying out a significant writing project. Teach them to find mentor texts and to learn from those texts, to set deadlines for themselves, to organize writing partnerships, to seek the sort of feedback that prompts revisions. That is, teach them to live their lives as writers.

Second graders come into our classrooms like first graders and leave like upperclassmen. This means that your teaching needs to stand on the shoulders of the previous years, taking children as far as they can go. And they can go far—especially if you rise to the potential of the second semester. For second graders who have grown up in writing workshops and especially for those who have grown up learning within *Units of Study for Primary Writing*, this yearlong trajectory can help your youngsters go further in both narrative and nonnarrative writing, and it can help them develop the confidence and competence they'll need to tackle the challenges that lie ahead.

WORKS CITED

Professional Books

Calkins, Lucy. 1990. *Living Between the Lines*. Portsmouth, NH: Heinemann.

Calkins, Lucy, et al. 2003. *Units of Study for Primary Writing: A Yearlong Curriculum*. 7 vols. Portsmouth, NH: *first*hand, Heinemann.

———. 2006. *Units of Study for Teaching Writing, Grades 3–5*. 6 vols. Portsmouth, NH: *first*hand, Heinemann.

Ray, Katie Wood. 1999. *Wondrous Words: Writers and Writing in the Elementary Classroom*. Urbana, IL: National Council of Teachers of English.

Taylor, Sarah Picard. 2008. *A Quick Guide to Teaching Persuasive Writing, K–2*. Portsmouth, NH: *first*hand, Heinemann.

Vygotsky, Lev. 1978. *Mind in Society: The Development of Higher Psychological Processes*. Cambridge, MA: Harvard University Press.

Children's Books

Baylor, Byrd. 1995. *I'm in Charge of Celebrations*. New York: Aladdin.

Boelts, Maribeth, and Noah Z. Jones. 2008. *Those Shoes.* Somerville, MA: Candlewick Press.

Brinckloe, Julie. 1986. *Fireflies!* New York: Aladdin.

Crews, Donald. 1996. *Shortcut.* New York: HarperTrophy.

Galdone, Paul. 1981. *The Three Billy Goats Gruff.* New York: Clarion.

Kellogg, Steven. 2002. *The Three Little Pigs.* New York: HarperTrophy.

London, Jonathan. 1998. *Hurricane!* New York: HarperCollins.

Rylant, Cynthia. 1982. *When I Was Young in the Mountains.* New York: E. P. Dutton.

———. 1997. *Poppleton.* New York: Blue Sky.

Yolen, Jane. 1987. *Owl Moon.* New York: Philomel Books.

Consider these other books in the

A QUICK GUIDE TO
Boosting English Acquisition in Choice Time, K–2
ALISON PORCELLI & CHERYL TYLER

Alison and Cheryl explain how choice-time workshops can be structured to help English language learners imagine, create, and explore language through play. They outline two units of study for choice-time workshops, the first using open-ended materials, the other using literature to inspire play.

A QUICK GUIDE TO
Teaching Persuasive Writing, K–2
SARAH PICARD TAYLOR

Children have voices that need to be heard and ideas that need to be understood. Building on this premise Sarah describes why you should try a persuasive writing unit of study, describes two units of study for the primary classroom, and lists tips and ideas for helping students get their persuasive writing out into the world.

Pocket-sized professional development on topics of interest to you.